My Limbs a Cradle, my Whisper a Song

poems by

Cathy Gilbert

Finishing Line Press
Georgetown, Kentucky

My Limbs a Cradle, my Whisper a Song

Copyright © 2024 by Cathy Gilbert
ISBN 979-8-88838-661-3 First Edition
All rights reserved under International and Pan-American Copyright Conventions. No part of this book may be reproduced in any manner whatsoever without written permission from the publisher, except in the case of brief quotations embodied in critical articles and reviews.

ACKNOWLEDGMENTS

A big thank you to the team at Finishing Line Press, especially to my editor Christen Kincaid, and also to many friends who read and offered feedback to poems in progress: Chelsey Hillyer, Jennifer Pauken, Richard Seehuus, and Michael Theune. And much gratitude to Joanne Diaz, whose invitation to a daily writing challenge helped me get back into a writing routine after becoming a mother.

Many of the poems in this collection were written in the dark, under the weight of sleeping infants—others were written in quiet snatches of time after visiting with my mother. None of those moments would be possible without the support of Cory Flanigan, who is not only an amazing papa to our children, but a formidable partner and loving husband to me. I'm grateful for his strength and encouragement, no matter the circumstance. And of course, a thank you to my children, Elliott and Jeannine, my daily inspiration and motivation.

Publisher: Leah Huete de Maines
Editor: Christen Kincaid
Cover Art: Michael Gilbert
Author Photo: Kessa Toland
Cover Design: Elizabeth Maines McCleavy

Order online: www.finishinglinepress.com
also available on amazon.com

Author inquiries and mail orders:
Finishing Line Press
PO Box 1626
Georgetown, Kentucky 40324
USA

Contents

Close Orbit 1

Visitation 2

Meteor Shower While the Twins Are Sleeping 4

A Better View 6

Baby Girl 7

Cleaning Bloodstains 8

On the Decline 9

Pulling the Clover 11

I Still Haven't Cried 12

Origin of Tears 14

At Play 15

Bullseye 16

To Be Needed 17

Nightly Sacrifice 18

New Momma's Lament 19

Our Work Is Never Done 20

I Miss You, Husband 21

Close of Day with Two Six-Month-Olds 22

Making the Soup 23

Grocery Store Prayer 24

Misophonia 26

Putting Away Christmas 28

What She Doesn't Know 29

More than a month now since my mother died 31

*For Mom, who taught me how to mother,
and for E and J, who made me one.*

Close Orbit

I asked the sonographer to repeat herself
because the earth shifted and fell out
from underneath me, the cold gel on my stomach
became the cold shock of space and I
grew anxious and dizzy and light.

Two weeks before, I had climbed the stairs
to the observatory—the telescope turned
to the rare sight of Jupiter and Venus so close
they could be held together in a single lens.
These bright orbs, caught in this moment
as a pair, floating side by side
in the round curve of glass I blinked through slowly.

They had been growing closer for months,
the pull of cosmic forces swirling them 'round
their orbits 'till one nearly lapped the other,
two playmates held in the darkness
of a mystic night sky.

               In the exam room,
I see them again, Jupiter and Venus
drawing near in the screen being turned
to ease my view. *Here is one,* she says,
and here is the other, the separate sacs
near black against the grainy white of my womb.
Two whole universes tucked inside, gravity pulls
doubly at my center, and I try to remember to breathe.

Visitation

After his death, my father
came to me in dreams.
The first time he was confused.
He came home and couldn't understand
why he didn't have the key,
why we'd given away his clothes.
He didn't know he was
supposed to be dead,
but he needed a belt,
so he strung an old rope
through the loops of his pants
and rummaged through the car trunk
for shoes.

           It's been many years now
since he's visited me. I thought,
perhaps, he'd finally realized
his state and moved on, made it across
whatever bright bridge or tunnel
one traverses to the other side.
It was bittersweet to think
those visits were gone.
And since having his grandchildren,
this boy who bears his name,
this girl who bears his face,
I've thought often of his absence:
how wide and big it grew
alongside my pregnant belly,
until his lack became its own shadow,
a grief hidden beneath the drowning joy
of having two babies at once who
won't meet the man who helped make me.

And yet, last night, on the eve
of the day of his own birth,
he rang a doorbell in my dreams.
When I answered, he stood before me
looking well and wearing all black,
a strange car in the driveway behind him.
I had both babes at my hips,
and asked if he had time to stay.
He looked unsure, confused again,
but said *I think I have a couple hours*
as if time was now a thing he couldn't measure,
seconds and eons all one.
His voice was clear and familiar
and I smiled to hear it, opened
the door wide to let him in.
I think I have a meeting later
he muttered as I nodded,
repositioned the children and said
a couple of hours is just fine.

Meteor Shower While the Twins Are Sleeping

I get up to see the Perseids
a little past two in the morning,
after I nurse both children again,
make sure they are soundly in their cribs.

I find batteries for the portable monitor,
slip into pants and shoes and carefully
close the back door behind me.

Silence. I imagine these were
the blissful moments for which my father
set the quiet alarm on his watch.
Each celestial event an opportunity,
a reason to rise from bed.

I can see him: alone, quiet, in slippers
standing on the back porch, gazing
up, up, up and praying for a clear night,
or that the clouds would pass to reveal
the lunar eclipse, or the conjunction
of planets with the moon, or the passage
of the space station across the dark sky.
His disappointment when the view was obscured.

Tonight, as I round the corner of the house,
walk out into the adjacent empty lot, I see
only the echoes of a few stars dulled
by cloud cover and the orange glow of a street lamp.

Thwarted, I return to bed with the humid air still
stuck to my skin, and I dream up what displays
of the night sky I will someday share
with the two who are breathing softly in their cribs.

And I hope that somewhere amongst those
orbiting bodies in galaxies beyond, my father
is rousing from slumber, gazing down, down, down,
praying for the clouds to part and for a chance
to see these two infant stars burning bright.

A Better View

Since birth, my son has loved
the window in the nursery,
the one facing the busy street,
with its strange noises ushered in
by cars and trucks and motorcycles.

Today is no different.
I hold him up to see the school bus
that stopped for our neighbor's daughter,
its lights blinking through the morning's light fog.

But moments later, when I put him down
and he protests the drudgery
of the nursery floor, when he crawls
to the window and pulls himself up,
I see him gain another inch of the view
as he teeters on his tip-toes,
a move he's not done before.

And my heart aches a little over each toe,
the precious curve of his foot,
and that newfound air floating there
just below the smooth skin of his heel.

Baby Girl

It was you, I think, in my dream,
floating above me, swaddled and warm.
You who spoke without speaking, told me
you would be with me in a year's time
and that all would be well.

In that dream, I pulled you
down to me, you ethereal thing,
a glow and lightness about you.
You fit into me, your head
found the nook where my arm
meets my shoulder. I remember,
still, the lowering of my eyes,
the resting of my cheek
on your forehead.
I remember still
the sense of peace.

In reality, you arrived
with an intensity
I could not control.
I had learned your weight over time,
yours and the weight of your brother—
you never said there'd be a brother,
vying for space behind my taut growing belly—

and when they told me to, I reached
my hands down, I pulled you up
to me, out of me, into my arms.
The blood stayed
under my fingernails
for three days.

You spoke in screams,
cries that pierced the air.
But your face: something in it
more familiar than family.
I knew I knew you, from before.

Cleaning Bloodstains

My mother taught me in the basement bathroom:
cold water will release the stain, hot water will set it.
I picked up the underwear I'd been soaking,
scrubbed soap into the blotchy red,
rubbed the cloth together and told myself
I'd watch the calendar better next month.

There in the basement, hidden away
from my father and brothers, I felt a little
disgust at the process of cleaning this mess,
a little sick as I twisted and wrung out
the dull panties. I'd wanted proof
of my womanhood without understanding
that proof often comes with a cost.

Now, after her fall, I clean bloodstains again:
first from the linoleum at the bottom of the stairs,
then from my mother's bathrobe and clothes,
the blood from a gash on her head
and the absence of anyone at home to watch her.
I soak the clothes in the tub, the cold water
quickly turning stains to snake-like trails
that wriggle away from the fabric
and dissipate into the water, now tinged pink.

Here is proof of what we've been
hiding from: she can't be alone.
My brother paces in the kitchen, mulling
over doctor's orders and calls to family.
But I sit with the blood.

On the Decline

After the tornado ripped through
I saw a child-sized mattress
in the middle of a corn field—
the remains of the harvested stalks had become
a flimsy bed frame for its tattered weight.

Seeing it so bare and alone, it wasn't hard
to think of the child who wasn't in it.
It wasn't hard to hope for safety
when the sunlight shone so clearly
on its emptiness, or see the way
the springs must have lifted
when the child fled for cover,
a small blanket perhaps in tow.

Just as, when the voice on the phone
said my mother had fallen again,
it wasn't hard to imagine that she too was safe,
wrapped in a hospital bed, some medicine
for the pain, perhaps an ice pack for the inevitable
bump on her head.

                      But the face that greets me now
is battered: one side puffy, purple, one eye
peering through bloodshot sclera and swollen skin.
She smiles, only half knowing why she is here.
She asks why her face feels strange, keeps
saying she sees sand on the hospital sheets,
and even when we tell her again and again
she has a black eye, ask her not to touch it
or the gash beaming through her eyebrow,
the image slips through her fingers.
She grasps again with questions, and fails.

Somewhere, the child who isn't
in the bed in the cornfield
is in the loving arms of parents,
protected and warm. But here,
seeing my mother and the way her shrinking
frame fills the thin sterile mattress,
I wonder what it would feel like
to have escaped the storm.

Pulling the Clover

Three weeks ago I thought the clover,
with its happy green leaves and tiny yellow petals,
would make a fine ground cover, a blanket
of living stalks, a reassurance, a softening.

Instead, it now threatens to strangle the roses,
its fast spread like a plague to the thorns
that can only be defense to those who reach for them
and whose flesh is soft enough for hurt.

And so I pull it, the clever clover, carefully,
though I still disturb the spiders, snails, and fleeing
roly-polies from the home they've made beneath.

Dirt gathers under my nails, I shake off
a tiny snail clinging to the doomed weeds,
and though the sky begins to drop soft rain
around me, I stay at my task.

A neighbor revs his lawn mower hoping
to beat the downpour. The cars on the street
zoom by, windshield wipers not yet engaged,
the glass slowly obscuring with little droplets.

If I sit here pulling long enough, perhaps
I won't have to think of the elderly friend slowly
dying of cancer whose birthday is today,
or the fact that my mother can't remember his name,
her own mind victim to the too quick decay of dementia.

Perhaps, if I can loosen the noose of clover
from 'round these roses, the sweet fragrance
of their opening blossoms will help me forget
the growing clouds, the rain, the water caught
in my lashes and the streaks down my face.

I Still Haven't Cried

It's been three days since
I walked my mother around the halls
of her care unit, held her hand,
took a deep breath and answered her.
Three days since she looked at me
and had to ask who I was,
three days since the woman who birthed me
and held me and gave me a name
couldn't recall our relation,
three days since her look of sheer surprise
at the idea of having a daughter at all.
And I still haven't cried.

Because I had to get home to make dinner.
Because the laundry needed to be moved
from washer to dryer to basket to washer again.
Because I had to go to that meeting, and that one too.
Because the bills had to get paid, groceries bought,
because the Christmas tree needed to be put away,
because the dishwasher and the loading and unloading.

Because the crayon scribbles on the wall,
and the food glued to the kitchen floor.
Because the twin toddlers I never sleep trained,
because their transformation into leeches at night,
all mouths and limbs and wiggles and weights
all tossing and turning and cheeks laid upon my chest.

Because the post-nasal drip I can't kick
because the drainage pools in my throat at night,
and I wake to cough, and I wake to resettle wailing babes,
and I wake to remember her look of surprise at
I'm your daughter, mom. Your daughter.
And I wake to lie here and think and wonder
at how those tears still haven't come, choked back,
hiding behind the preparations for her birthday party,
which kind of tea sandwiches to make and how

many kinds of fruit to dip into chocolate
and what kinds of tea, and teacups and plates
and I wake until sleep comes again under the limbs of my children.

And in the morning, when I cough to clear my throat,
and I shake off the bleary night, perhaps I can shake
those tears loose or at least find the time to think
about them, slowly welling in my eyes, and the funny way
one can drown in such a small amount of water.

Origin of Tears
For Jeannine

Your first cries were tearless,
coming from fear, not pain.
Straight from the womb
you called out, a breath, a scream,
another breath, a wail, and there
in my arms you were comforted.

Later came tears, small drips
and streaks when you bumped
your head, your foot, your mouth.
Tears at night, lonely, hungry,
tears when I left for work
or for the other room.
Tears at well-meaning strangers,
at excited relatives and their pets.
Tears when I plucked
the broken bowl from your fingers,
when your brother ripped
a toy from your hands.
Tears when I put you down
before you were ready.
Your face shining, wet,
now harder to calm.

But I want you to know,
and I promise this is true,
that tears can also spring from joy.
You can see them here and here
on my cheeks as I watch you now
step once, twice, then three, four times
away from me, across the nursery, casually,
as if you have done it many lifetimes before.

At Play
For Elliott

My infant son plays
with a wooden train,
its use and real life
inspiration unknown to him.
He is too young
to worry about which
toys are meant for boys,
for girls. He plays equally
well with dolls or cars.
He is most interested
in the tags on the play mat
or the layer of dust
under the dresser.

Watching him now, engine
held in his small grip,
it is not about snips and snails
or sugar and spice;
it's about the wonder
he must feel as he lifts
its heft, touches the grain
of the wood with his palm,
eyes the stack of the steam engine
and places it, nipple like, in his mouth.

Bullseye

Tonight I understand the Amazons
and their willingness to cut off a breast,
a sacrifice made so that the arrow
would never miss its deadly mark.

After an hour of nursing two babes to sleep,
the sucking and pulling, the scratching
and twisting and twiddling and pinching,
I dream of removing my own breasts

leaving them there in the bed for my children
to cuddle and pet. And yet, away from them,
body once again my own, likely I would miss
the way those tiny mouths always find their target

even in the dark, even in their sleep,
the dark nipple a bullseye, fragrant with milk.

To Be Needed

I caught my breath tonight
at the sight of blood, my son's,
crusted into his tiny fingernail,
a bright red stain trickling
into the crease of his
ring- and middle-fingers.
Looking closer, it was nothing really,
perhaps a hangnail torn,
or a cuticle caught and pulled back.
I took a warm cloth and wiped him clean.
No worse for wear.

Later, I read a story of a woman,
only 21 years old, who died in a fire
today in her home. A hero, they called her:
she saved her 12 day old infant
by strapping the child into a car seat
and dropping it to the ground
from a second story window.
The tragedy, her sacrifice, her choice,
unspeakable.

                      My son's bloodied finger
seems a blessing now. A hurt
I can still comfort.
Tonight when my children wake,
when they cry out afraid or hungry
I won't hesitate to go to them,
won't resent their inability to sleep
through the night. Why resent it
when to be needed and to fulfill that need
are joys I'm privileged to keep living?

Nightly Sacrifice

Each night I am sacrificed,
sleeping with each arm splayed out
away from my body, a letter T,
a cross. Two little humans
rest at my chest, their soft snores
and vulnerable weight a trap.
They wake every few hours,
mouths roving in search
of the milk they are sleeping on.

Someday, I'm told, I will remember
these moments fondly, cherish them
for the sacred nighttime rituals they are.
But for now, I can't help but notice
the crick in my neck, the numbness in my arms,
or the overwhelming urge I feel to turn away
and sleep on my side,
the blanket pulled high to my neck.
I can't help but wish for the little space
that will someday feel much too large.

New Momma's Lament

I want to want to say
yes to you, dear husband,
want to want your proposition
how you lean into me
how you press your hips
how the pressure of you
the pressure of the months between
lingers as you pull back

I want to want you, want
to feel a stirring
to feel electric
to feel synapses awake
fire into ready, meet you
here, anywhere until
the quiet falls from lips

I want to want it, you
I want to see how to want you
I will, I think, I hope
want again, but
tiny fingers
helpless toes
and suckling mouths
but language forming
and knees pulled up for crawling
and feet planted to stand
but tears and giggles
piss and shit and piss and shit again
but play play play

and all the want I want
is metered out, increments
of affection building to quota
and it's spent and I'm spent
and they you me all want
more

Our Work Is Never Done

It's a poet's job to notice:
the slant of light
or snowy woods
or a lonely cloud.
But some days there is nothing
to report, our heads and eyes
too busy with the work
of living to notice anything
past the fingers of our hands.

As now, at close of day,
I can't get past
the dishes dormant
in the sink, the laundry
whirring in the basement,
the sleepy weight
tugging at my lids,
or the anticipation hanging
like earrings at my lobes
as I wait for the first cry
of the night to pierce
through the monitor,
my limbs a cradle,
my whisper a song.

I Miss You, Husband

Today, I caught just a glimpse
of the inside of your finger,
a spot in the middle where a blister
had already worn its way
into your skin, burst, and healed enough
that new pink skin peeked
out from under a layer half gone.

There was a time
when I would have known
that spot intimately, noticed it
the day it first appeared,
felt it against my own fingers
as we clasped hands, seen it
while you chopped vegetables
or stirred the pan, touched it
lovingly as we lounged.
There was a time I had time
to be a part of its healing.

But now we are occupied
with the raising of small people,
our hands filled with their wriggling,
instead of each others'.
I am not sorry for their intrusion,
with their tiny feet and large cries,
but I am sorry for the chance I missed
to wish you and your finger well.

Close of Day with Two Six-Month-Olds

My mother's recipe for banana bread
sits on the counter. It's been there
since morning, and it still smells of good
intentions and the hope that time
would open up somehow and allow
for butter and flour, sugar and heat.

Someday in the future, when the children
aren't crying from the nursery floor,
frustrated at their lack of mobility,
when there are no more diapers
to be forgotten in the washer,
in need of another rinse,
when the exhaustion doesn't drip
so heavily from my head and arms,

I might long for these days of coos
and giggles and smiles which reset
the air each morning with the sun.
But now, after nightfall, I only long
for my mother's banana bread,
sliced thick and slathered in cold butter,
and the time to eat it warm.

Making the Soup

Somewhere, not long after roasting the squash,
chopping the onions and garlic and ginger,
the big pieces of apple, somewhere after
curry powder sizzles in butter,
and the chopped pieces are tossed in,
and each begins to glisten and sing,
somewhere after the steam rises
from the hollowed shells of butternut,
its orange flesh added to the pot,
the sticky bits licked from my fingers,
my husband's, my children's,
and water is poured, and everything is stirred,
somewhere before it's all whipped through a blender,
before the table is set, before the timer rings
for the rolls, having risen fat and golden
in the oven's dense heat, before pepper
is added with the crank of a grinder to our bowls,

there is a moment where the bubbling sheen
of the soup's surface is pure golden light.
The spoon is removed, the liquid still whirling,
and no one moves. Each with a child in our arms,
my husband and I stand over the stove,
all of us staring, not wanting to disturb
as the cloud of steam rises into the oven vent
and the seconds tick away on the timer
and the world and all its terrors disappear
because here in front of us is magic, pure
and golden, and all we need do is consume it.

Grocery Store Prayer

I hear the whine
sailing from the check out
to the back of the store.
Not my child.

My children are home,
playing with their grandmother,
while I stand here
in the vegetable aisle
listening to some other child
throw a fit, listening to the mother
speak of home, of bed.

My children are home,
happily yelling out
their "dadas" and "babas,"
happily stacking blocks
and picking themselves up
after each little tumble,
while I stand here
hoping the cereal in the cart
will appease them
in the morning, hoping
the days of whining
in the grocery store
can be put off a bit longer,

and hoping that someday
when it *is* my child
whose whine carries
to the produce aisle,
that perhaps some other mother
will be struck by the sound,
its familiar drone,
and after a grimace,
she'll put off judgment
and send a little prayer

for my sanity,
as I do now for her:
my hands on the cart
a quiet blessing.

Misophonia

My mother was bothered
by mouth sounds: smacking
lips, crunching too loud,
spoons hitting teeth. She
hated superfluous sniffing, too.
I learned to eat potato chips
in another room, or else
hear her exasperation.
Do you have to eat so loudly?

Once in a common room
in grad school, where I sat
eating my lunch, a fellow student
claimed no one could crunch as loudly
as me, unless they were trying.
The shame of my childhood
rose up, burning my face.
My mother seemed so near.

I don't know why, then,
I was surprised to hear her
today, in my own voice.
*The sound of you grinding
your teeth hurts my head*
I said to my four-toothed son,
who was discovering the way
teeth felt raked across each other,
echoing in the small cave
of his mouth.

        I'd meant *heart*,
as I cringed for the health
of his nascent enamel,
but *head* is the word that leapt
from my tongue, so trained
by remarks heard throughout
the meals of my childhood.

I wanted to take them back,
those words, but knowing I can't,
I add them to the list of growing proof
of how easy it is to become the parents
we didn't know we didn't want to be.

Putting Away Christmas

There's not much to it, really.
No hordes of lights to be balled up,
tangled for next year's exhuming.
No holiday tablecloths to be folded,
nor tinsel to mix with dead needles,
waiting to be swept up and discarded.

It's only a shoebox
that needs to be filled
with my childhood ornaments
which adorn our tree. Our children
are too young to have made
their own. That time will come.

For now I have this shoebox,
which my mother gave me
long before she forgot
where these things are kept.
Before she forgot what day it was
her sisters' names
my husband's name
which grandchild she is talking to
the fact that her aunts are dead
what the shirt is doing in her hand
how to flush a toilet
how to put a barrette in her hair
how to bake her famous cookies
or the coffee cake
or the manicotti my nephew ate
so much of when he was still so small.

Before she forgot that she forgot
all of this, she gave me this shoebox
filled with my childhood ornaments,
the fragile ones wrapped in tissue.
I put them away carefully because
I know it's all more fragile now.

What She Doesn't Know

My mother knows something has happened.
She knows that her son looked at her that way,
concerned, not panicked, eyebrows curved down
toward the center of his nose—so like his father's.
She knows that he asked her *Are you alright?*
and that she said *yes*.

                There was a glass of water provided,
a hand on her shoulder. There was a blackness that lifted,
a few seconds wiped clean and taken away.
There was a distorted face, hers; there was
a chair, plush, cushioning her body, her arms.

Next day, she knows she sits with head in hands,
soft; she knows there is lightness, she knows
she holds still and waits. She knows she is scared.
She knows the MRI is coming, Monday is it?,
and that they are looking for something they might
never find. She knows she can't drive. She pantomimes
driving like they do in the old movies, the wheel
turned back and forth, as if going left and right,
left and right, is the only way to keep a straight line.

She knows that I am sitting and listening to her,
that I smile, my eyes do not, and I keep asking
yes, but how do you feel today? She knows that
this coffee is good, that the pizza is coming.
She knows all this,

                but she doesn't know
the fear her confusion strikes into my heart,
the sadness I will sleep with tonight
and wake up with come morning. How I observe
the tremble of her hand as she talks in circles.
She doesn't know the tears I've shed at this
gradual loss of her, the letters and journals
I should never have read, the questions I can't ask

for fear of the answers or the distinct lack of them,
the memories I choose to keep of my father,
or the selection I am making
now and tomorrow and the next day
of memories I prefer to keep of her.

More than a month now since my mother died

and today my shit smells like hers.
That familiar reek rising up
like the smells she unearthed as a child
on the family farm. Blackened fingernails
digging in the the vegetable garden,
roots reaching for the layer of humus.
The scent of cow pies across the fence.
The tang of the pig shit her sister once slipped in.

But it's not just shit, no, it's a smell mixed
with my sweat and my womanhood
and the shift in the air of menstrual blood
soon to be spilled. Sex and bacteria.
Her microbiome seeded into mine, the smell
of her excrement and blood hardwired in me.

Today my shit smells like my mother's,
and my nose is an olfactory guide
to a montage of intimate spaces:
I am a child, unwilling to let her
out of my sight for five minutes.
I am a teen, passing toilet paper to her,
or her to me, under the stall in a public restroom.
I am a young woman, entering the family bathroom
just after my mother has used it.
I am an adult, waiting to help her clean herself:
her dominant hand burned badly, wrapped
in a bandage she should not get wet.

Today my shit smells like my mother's,
the woman whose pulses I rode in on like waves,
and I am thinking of the first sound a baby hears,
its first lullaby. Most say it's the mother's heartbeat,
ignoring that other organs make noise too:
the stomach gurgles, gas moves through the bowels.
Surely as I exited my mother's womb, I heard
the organs of her nethers in between

the muffled screams of her labor.

Today, my shit smells like my mother's.
And soon, I will clean myself and flush it away,
but for a moment longer, I will sit with this pungent specter
and breathe.

Cathy Gilbert received her MA from the Master of Arts Program in the Humanities at the University of Chicago. She now lives in Central Illinois where she is a Professor of English at Heartland Community College and mother to twins. She teaches her students about academic and creative writing, but her children teach her about imagination and word play. She writes poetry and creative non-fiction, through which she has explored her family history, the La Brea tar pits, fleeing a foreign country in the beginning of a pandemic, and now the depths of motherhood and the mother-daughter relationship. Her poems and essays have previously appeared in *Hobart, decomP, Peoria Magazine,* and *Motherly.*

www.ingramcontent.com/pod-product-compliance
Lightning Source LLC
Chambersburg PA
CBHW022044080426
42734CB00009B/1229